Shadow & Light

Photography of Gary Rea

Copyright 2015 by Gary Rea

I was born in Oklahoma City in 1952 and the first camera I ever had was given to me by my father when I was about 4 or 5 years old. It was a Kodak Brownie Hawkeye that used roll film and I had to crank the film forward after each shot. As young as I was, I was unaware of this when my father and I went to Fort Sill, in Lawton, Oklahoma one day, so all my shots of WWI and WWII cannon and other military equipment on display there were double exposures. Thus, my very first photographs were abstracts, though not intentionally so, of course.

Later, at 18, when I didn't even have a camera, I started reading issues of Popular Photography, thinking I'd like to become a photographer. It was at this same time that I was out of high school and needed a job and wasn't going to college yet, so I needed some way to avoid being drafted and sent to Vietnam with the Army or Marines. At that time, Nixon was President and troop withdrawals had already begun. Thus, the Air Force and Navy were no longer sending recruits to Vietnam.

Since I couldn't swim to save my life, I decided the Navy was not the place for me, and I got a brochure from the Air Force, instead. It was also the first time in history that new recruits were allowed to choose what field they wanted to train for, so, looking through the brochure of job categories, the only one that appealed to me and that had some potential for training me for something useful in civilian life was photography. I enlisted, thinking they'd make me a photographer, of course, but I wound up as a Still Photographic Laboratory Specialist - a photo lab technician - instead.

This actually worked out for the best, as the Air Force had segregated the two functions and so the photographers only shot pictures, but lacked the in-depth laboratory training I received, and conversely, I was left out of the in-depth camera training the photographers got. However, this didn't hinder my ability to teach myself that side of the field on my own time. In fact, I probably benefitted from learning on my own, where the camera was concerned, as it freed me to learn from the then "modern masters" of the day and to experiment with in-camera techniques that I probably wouldn't have been trained for by the Air Force.

Meanwhile, being trained as a lab technician and doing that as my daily work prepared me in ways I didn't realize fully at the time. I could see how the two functions were an integrated whole and that most of the work being done by those modern masters of photography was mostly being accomplished in the lab, as opposed to in the camera. The camera was only the starting point. In those days of film, as it is today in digital photography, the initial "image capture," as people call it these days, was only the beginning and it was in the darkroom, during processing of the film and the exposure and processing of the print, that the final image was arrived at. Thus, all the greatest photographs ever made in the era of film were created, not so much as the result of good camera technique, but as the result of manipulation of the film, and especially the print, in the lab. In those days, the final image *was* the print. Today, of course, the final image is a digital file and the darkroom has been replaced by digital software that emulates darkroom techniques and the effects of those techniques.

As for those digital emulations of lab techniques, I use Nik Software's Silver Efex Pro 2, a plugin for Photoshop and Lightroom, which I host in Lightroom 4.0. It is the best digital emulation of black and white lab techniques I'm aware of. It allows me to fully explore the effects of such laboratory printing techniques as dodging and burning and it also allows me to explore the effects of push-processing of film, as well. So, I have full control over the final image and this was the main frustration I had during the era of film.

When I say I was frustrated, I mean that back when the final image was the print, you had to have full control over the entire process, from camera to finished print. If you didn't, then you lost control over what your images looked like. All the greatest photographers of the era of film were accomplished lab technicians as well as cameramen, or they at least were able to afford to rely on the services of expert lab technicians to complete their prints, or, like the Magnum photographers, had these services provided for them. The best among them, though, were those who did their own lab work. They had complete control over what they were producing. We're talking about people like Ansel Adams, Minor White, Brett Weston, et al, in other words, the f/64 Group; the photographers who invented the "Zone System."

While I was in the Air Force and had access to the lab, I had that same level of control over my images, although I hadn't yet reached my mature stage as a photographer, so I wasn't able to make the most of what I had access to. After I left the Air Force, in 1974, I was then left with no control over my final image at all. I was, for all intents and purposes, just like most other amateur photographers, in that, I could only control the image as far as what happened in the camera. Once I surrendered my film to whatever lab I was using (and I couldn't afford a custom lab, at that time), usually via the local drugstore, like everyone else, I had absolutely no control over what happened to the images I'd shot. They would be machine processed and printed for the "correct" exposure, no matter what my original intent had been. Thus, oftentimes, my intent was completely lost in the process and I wound up with nothing resembling what I had originally envisioned. Things remained this way until the advent of digital photography.

But, even with the advent of digital photography, I was still frustrated by the lack of image quality, as compared to that of film. By the time digital camera sensors were not only equal to film, but surpassing it in terms of image quality, I was ready.

While many photographers are going back to shooting film and many new photographers who got started with digital photography are now shooting film, I have already been there, myself, and will never go back again. I see no point to it. I believe digital technology has been the biggest improvement in photography since its invention over 150 years ago. There is now the capability to create silver gelatin prints from digital images, and this is the direction I want to go in, moving forward. While the digital image is an advancement and so is digital image processing, the end product sought by serious collectors will always be the print and, where that is concerned, inkjet and giclee prints simply won't do, as they are a form of printing technology, not actual photographs, as silver gelatin prints are. Then there is the issue of longevity and, where that is concerned, I don't believe there is a case for inkjet and giclee, yet, as the technology is simply too new. Where silver gelatin is concerned, though, it has a long history and is a trusted photographic print medium.

I began shooting street photography exclusively in 2012, and shortly thereafter, exclusively for black and white. I began shooting only for black and white because I believe color to be a distraction and because black and white has long been the standard of fine art photography.

While color has become accepted as legitimate in fine art photography, it took some forty years for it to achieve that status. When I say that color is a distraction, I am referring to the fact that bright colors, especially reds and yellows, tend to draw the eye away from the subject, especially if the subject is drab or monochromatic and, if it *is* monochromatic, then why bother using color at all?

Many street photographers carry a camera with them at all times, in order to be ready to shoot whatever they might encounter, but I have a feeling that many of them are only shooting while they are doing other things, like shopping or going to the dentist. I have a more disciplined approach, I believe, which consists of going out daily and deliberately devoting my full attention to shooting, for two or three hours, or until both my batteries are exhausted, whichever comes first. During these sessions, I look for areas of deep shadow broken by shafts of light, first and foremost. Secondly, I am looking for architectural details that look interesting and work with the shadow and light to create an interesting backdrop or environment for shooting. The last element I look for is foot traffic through this space and, when I find the combination of all these factors in the same place at the same time, I will typically spend from several minutes to as much as half an hour shooting multiple versions of the scene with different people.

It doesn't matter to me who is there, what they look like, what sex they are, etc. All I'm looking for is the human element to complete the scene and it's the scene - not the people - that is the subject. A lot of people, including artists and art lovers, have a hard time with understanding this. They have been trained, all their lives, to believe that in any scene in which there is a human being, the person is always the subject matter. But, there are many examples of street scenes in which the people are mere props, just elements that complete the scene. If you examine, for example, Paul Strand's 1915 photo of people on Wallstreet in New York City, the people are silhouettes, seen from a distance. No one in that scene is any more the "subject" of the scene than anyone else is. I have many scenes I've shot like this around Seattle and it's the same thing with those. There is no one in the photo who is intended as subject matter. Even when I'm shooting a single individual on the street, they are usually anonymous, sometimes because their face is obscured by shadow, or because they are entirely in silhouette. This is completely intentional, as I have absolutely no interest whatsoever in the people in my scenes. I don't select the people, nor do I look for people to photograph.

This approach differs greatly from that of many street photographers these days. There are many who regard street portraits as street photography and there are others who believe the purpose of street photography is to document the human condition or to document humanity. These people, as far as I am concerned, are not doing street photography at all. They are doing portraiture, photojournalism or travel photography, but they are not street photographers. Street photography is, first of all, candid photography, thus, this rules out street portraits, entirely. It also rules out a lot of documentary photography, which isn't usually candid, either. As for documenting anything at all, my purpose is to create art. It's about achieving imagery that is abstract or surreal in some way. It isn't about chronicling the lives of people. That's the objective of photojournalism and I believe this invasion of street photography by portraitists and photojournalists is ruining and obscuring what real street photography is supposed to be. We're now at the point at which there are self-appointed street photography pundits putting out online "street photography" publications that regularly interview and feature the work of photojournalists and portrait photographers, and there are so-called "street photography" exhibitions and competitions that include anything but street photography. It's no wonder the public, if they've ever heard of street photography, in the first place, is confused about what it is. There are portrait photographers and photojournalists posing as street photographers who believe that street photographers should ask permission of people to photograph them! This is the antithesis of candid photography.

A couple of other differences between myself and other photographers are my use of the portrait, or vertical, format most of the time, and the fact that I don't title my images and, if forced to give a title, I always choose "Untitled." Where the portrait format is concerned, there are some good reasons I have for using it most of the time. First of all, if you're shooting photos for publication, then most of the time, you'll want to shoot for a full-page, just in case that is needed or preferred by an editor. Most magazines and books are published with pages that are in portrait format, so shooting for that format makes my images instantly usable as full-page illustrations. Another factor is that I tend to shoot a lot of layered imagery, in which things are stacked vertically, so the format lends itself to this, as well as to shooting full-length photos of people. In addition, when my work is included in an exhibition, portrait format images lend themselves well to conservation of wall space, as more of them can be put on a wall side by side than if you're dealing with hanging a group of images in landscape format. I do use landscape format when it suits the scene or my ideas, but, most of the time, I find myself habitually raising the camera to my eye in vertical orientation.

About the issue of titling my work, I resist using titles for my images, as I believe it leads the viewer's mind to a preconceived conclusion about the image and I prefer that my images speak for themselves. I intend no meaning and I am not "telling stories" with my images, so whatever meaning or significance someone derives from my work is entirely their own creation, not mine. I don't really care what people's reactions to my images are, so long as they have a reaction. There is nothing more insulting to me than someone taking a quick glance at an image and then moving on to the next one. I prefer that the viewer spend some time with each image and that it stirs an emotional response of some sort. I don't care if they love it or hate it, as long as they feel something about it. I prefer that people wonder about and puzzle over my images and I believe that an image that is immediately readable or understandable without further thought or consideration is probably not a great image, as it cannot hold the viewer's attention. On that note, I hope that I am successful in holding your rapt attention with the contents of this book and I thank you for buying it.

Gary Rea

August 2015

Westlake Series

The series included here are not complete, by any means and consist of only a few select images from each, due to space restrictions. Please contact me for inquiries about them. The Westlake Series was shot over a period of months in 2015 and is on-going. These are eight of the best examples from the series to date, which are all shot at a particular spot along the east side of Westlake Center mall, immediately beneath the Monorail track along 5th Avenue, between Pine Street and Olive Street in downtown Seattle. The attractive feature, for me, is the mix of shadow and light that occurs in late morning as the sun comes in high from the left and casts the shadow of the Monorail track on the sidewalk between the Monorail's support columns and the columns supporting the façade of Westlake Center. This shadow then combines with the shadows on the people and it is the combination of these shadows with the random illumination of parts of the people's bodies as they pass through this space that I find intriguing. There is an interplay between those parts of their form that become silhouetted against the column in the background and the illuminated portions of their form. The lines of the architectural backdrop impose a further relationship between figure and ground that acts both as a frame within a frame and as an element that interplays with the human form.

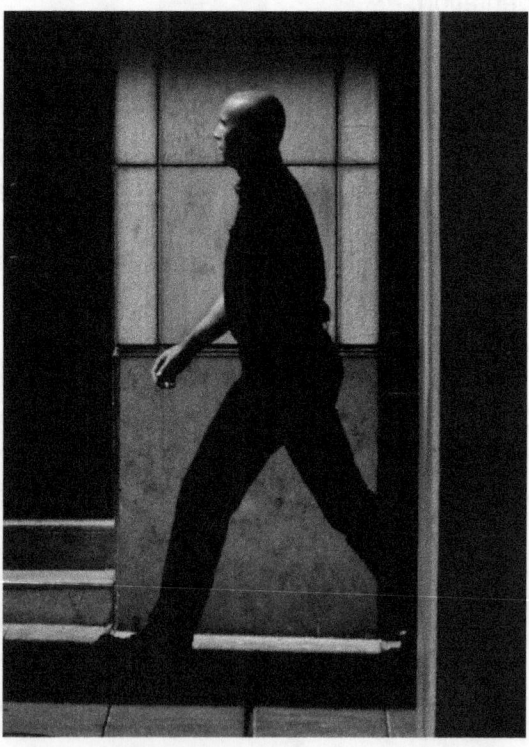 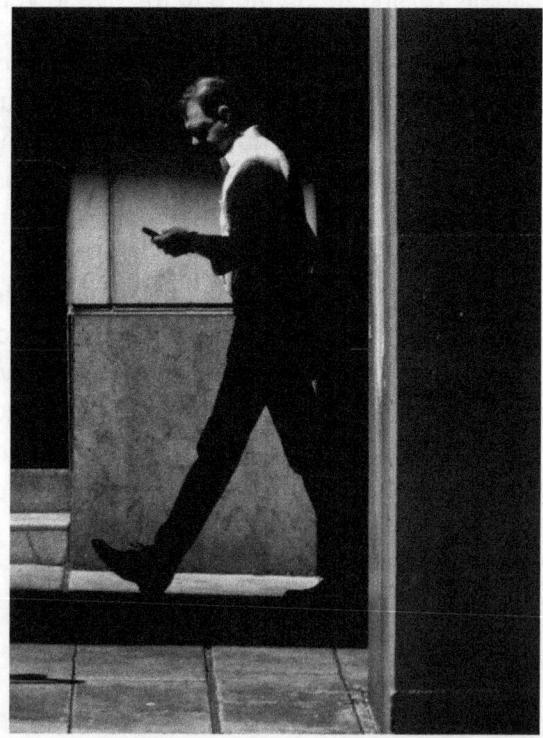

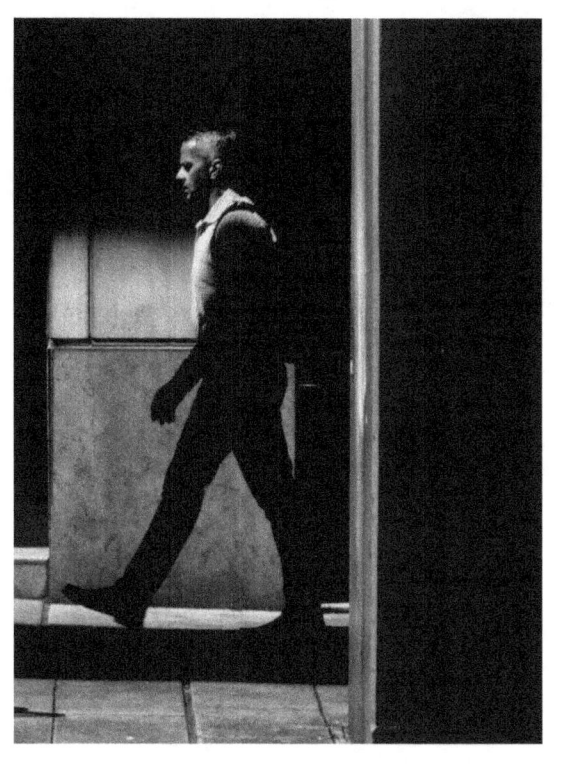
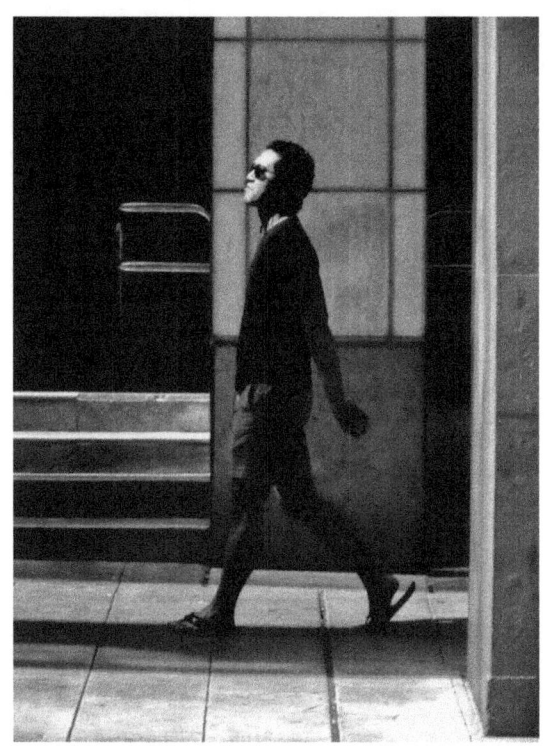
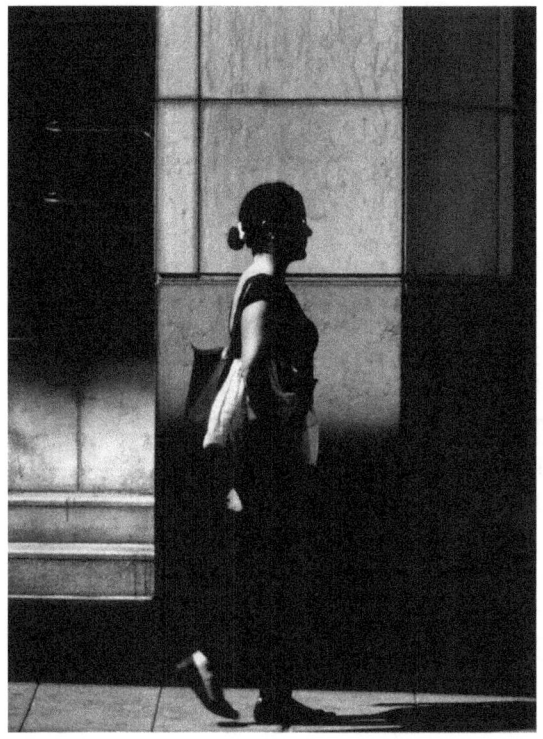
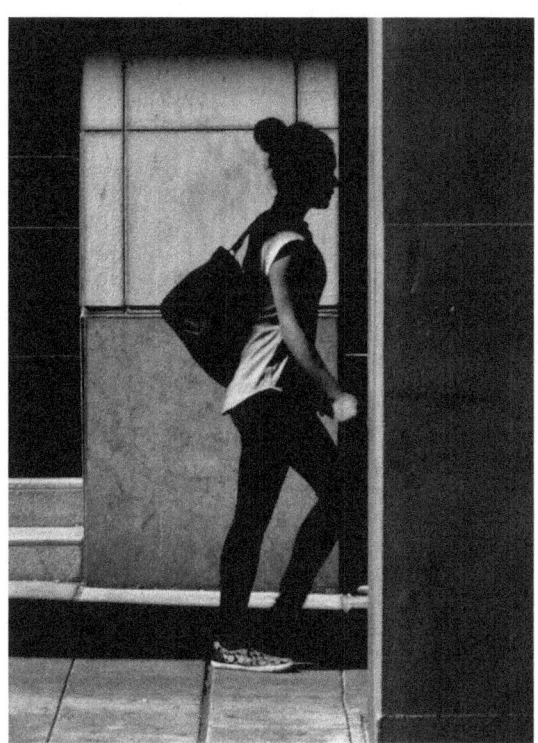

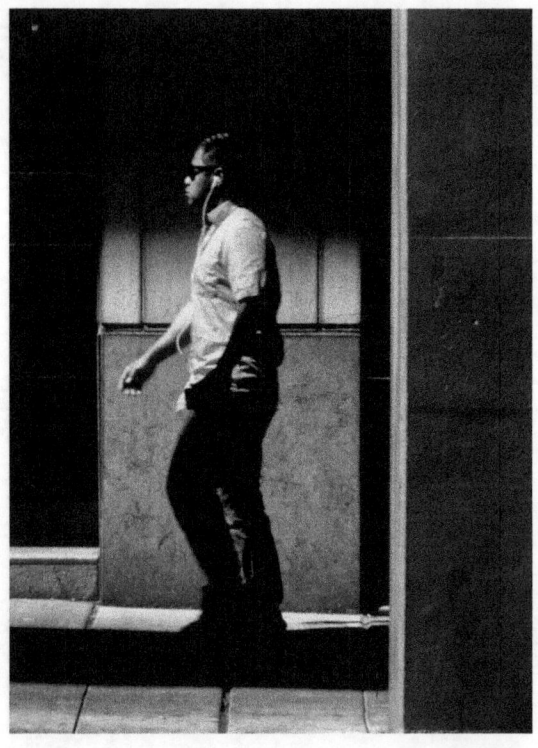 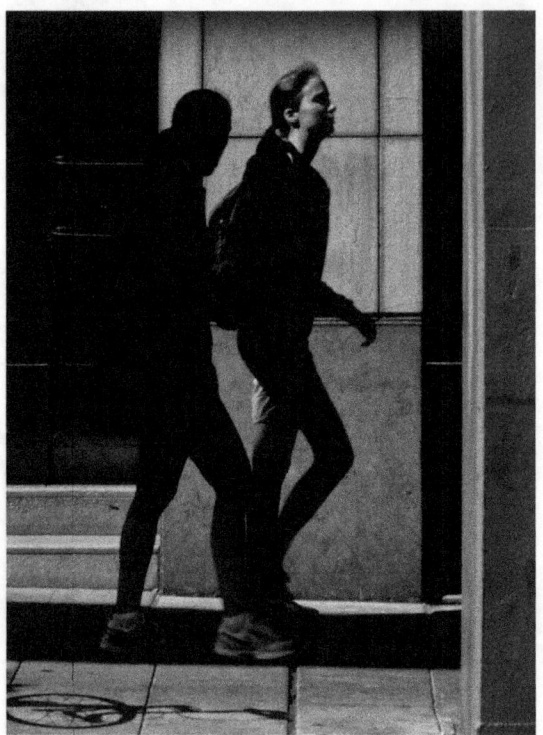

5th Avenue & Olive St. Series

There is an urban park between Stewart and Olive Streets and between the Westlake trolley line and 5th Avenue that is adjacent to Westlake Center mall. From the corner of Olive and 5th Avenue, looking west, I have been shooting a view of the corner of The Studios juxtaposed with one of the Monorail columns, off and on, for a number of months during 2015. My objective here is to capture the effects of the light and shadow falling on the people as they pass through the space in front of The Studios. Seen from my vantage point, the afternoon light falling across the pavement between the shadow of the Monorail column and the corner of the building The Studios is located in forms a zone of light with a hard-edged shadow beside it and the interplay of the light and the shadow upon the people passing through here creates some intriguing silhouettes and partial silhouettes. These are a few of the better images in this series.

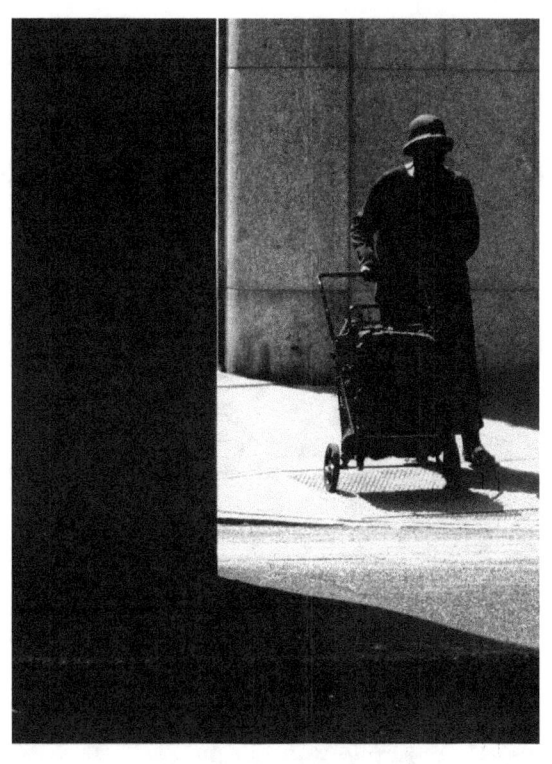
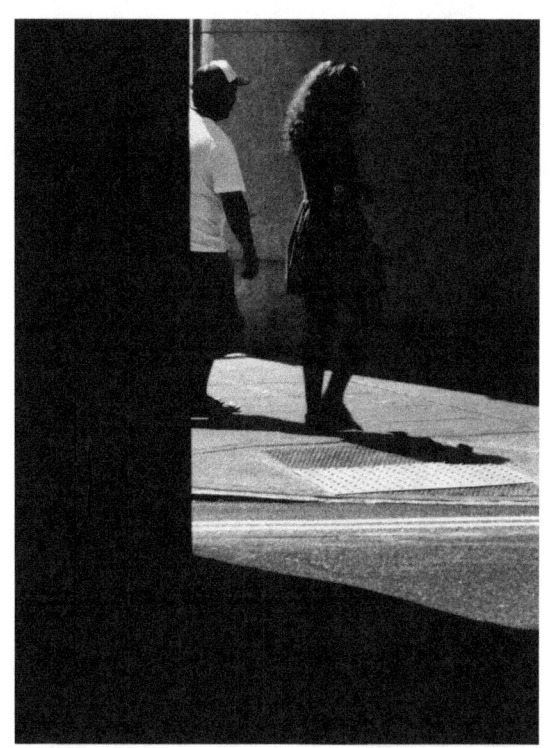
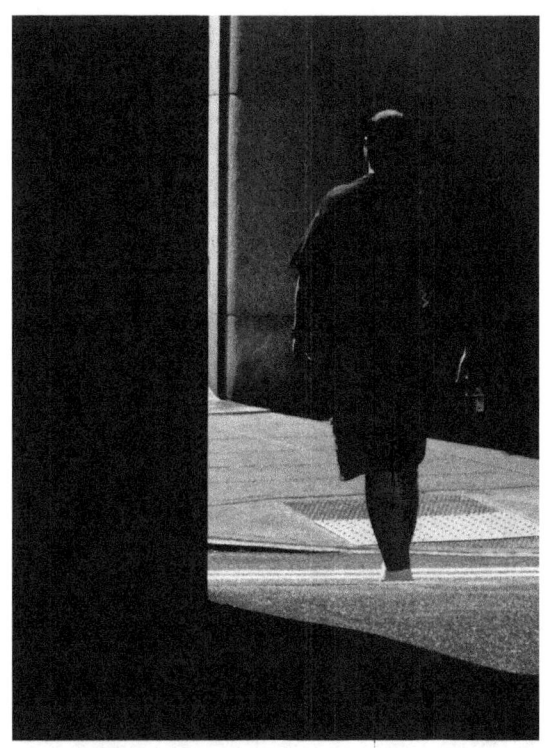
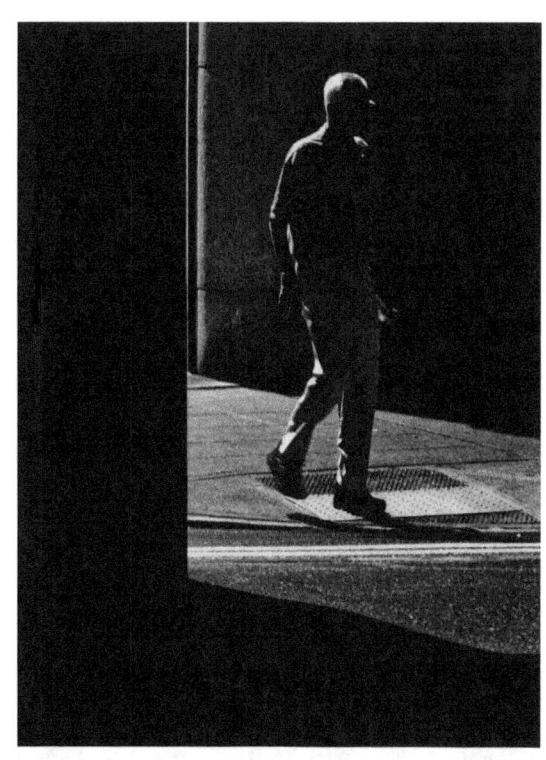

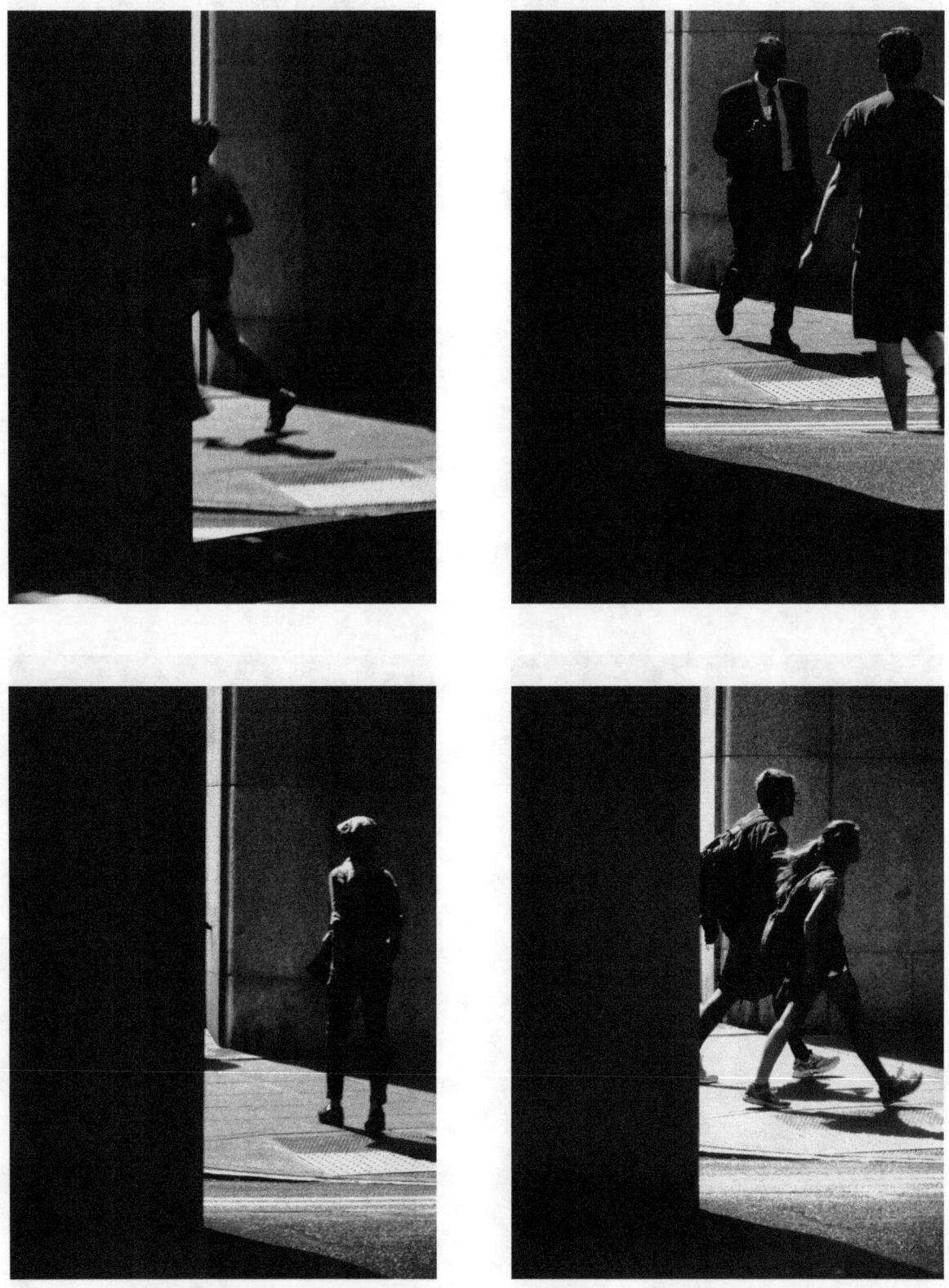

Blanchard Series

This is a series I have been working on since early 2015, named for Blanchard Street in the Belltown area of downtown Seattle. It consists of a view looking east up the hill at the centerline of Blanchard Street from the center median in Elliott Avenue, using a 360mm focal length. The telephoto view compresses the distance between the west and east sides of Western Avenue where it intersects with Blanchard. The intriguing aspect of this scene is how this view shows the people crossing Blanchard at Western, going either north or south on Western. It is the lighting and the juxtaposition of elements that I find compelling and the occasional addition of cars on the uphill slope add to the effect. Also, when people are passing through the scene on both sides of Western at the same time, the relative difference in apparent scale between them causes a form of forced perspective that makes the people nearer to my camera appear as giants in comparison to the people across the street from them and this adds a further surrealistic element to the scene. Again, these are some of the representative images in the series.

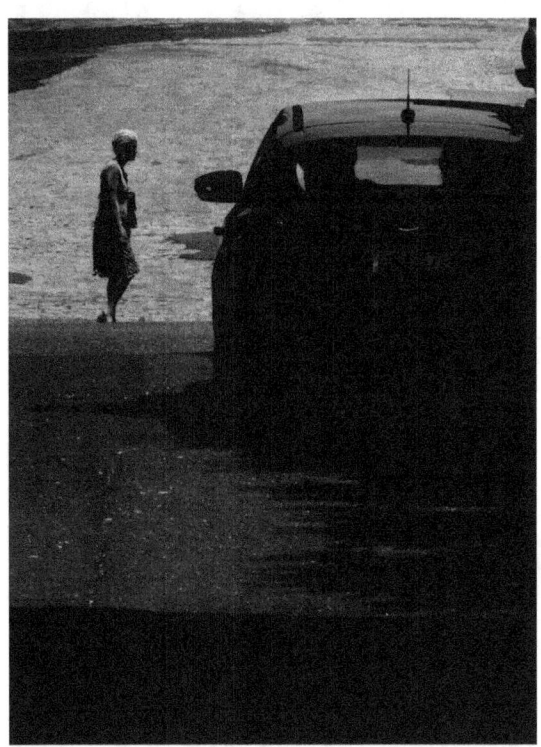
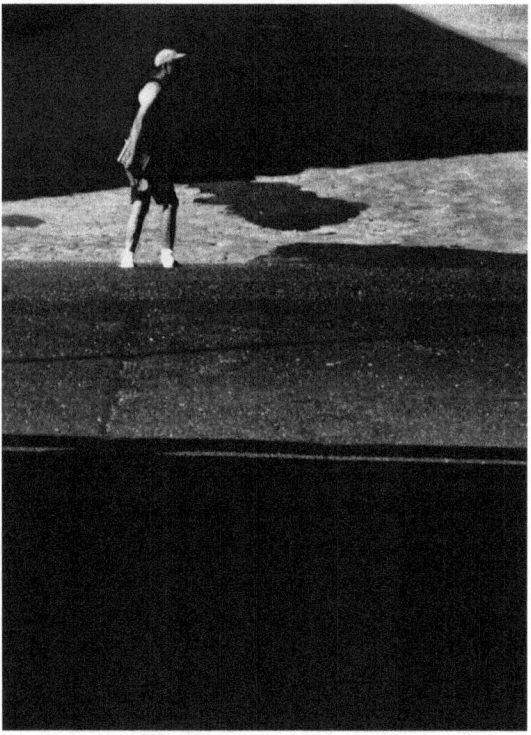

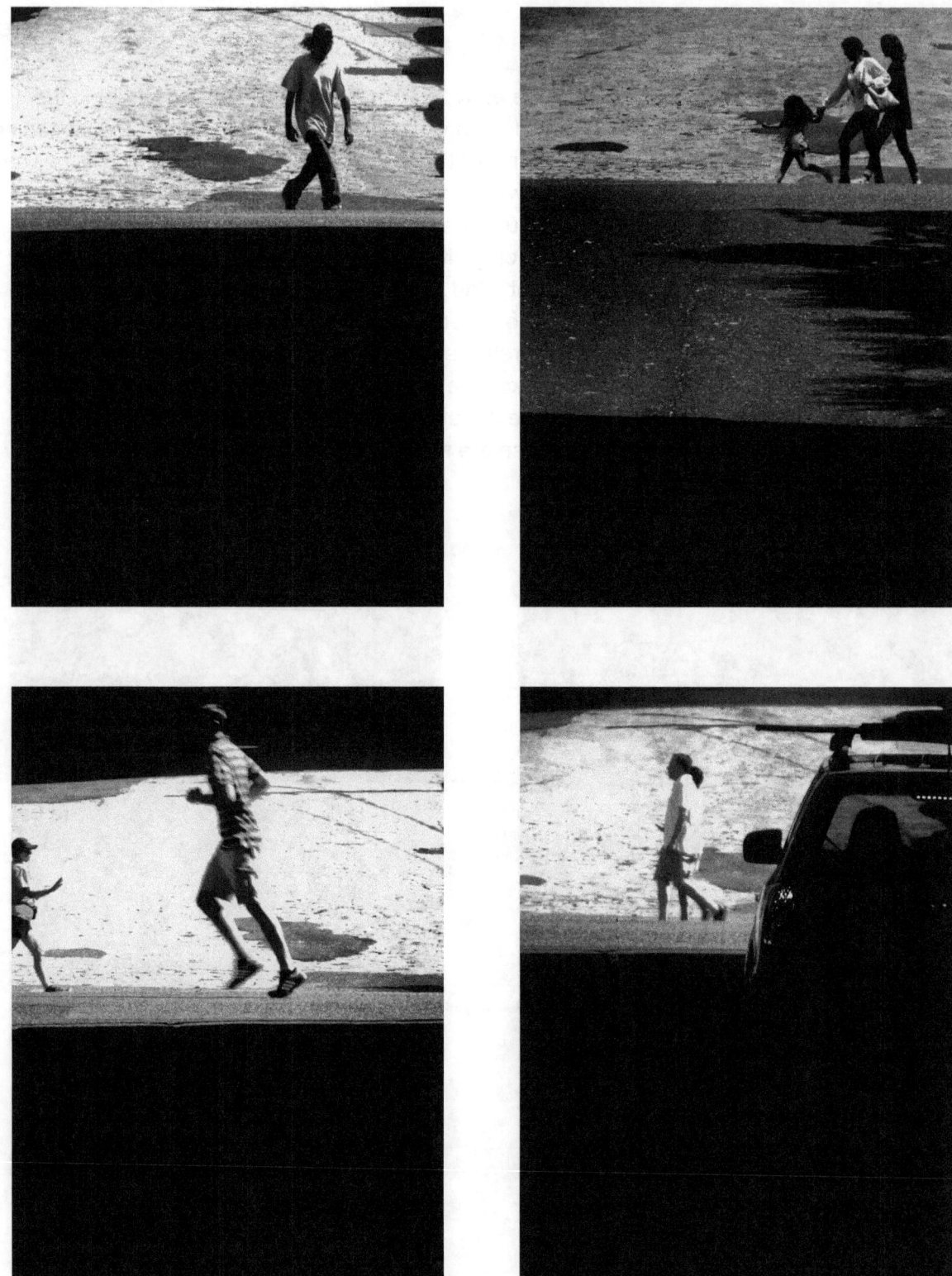

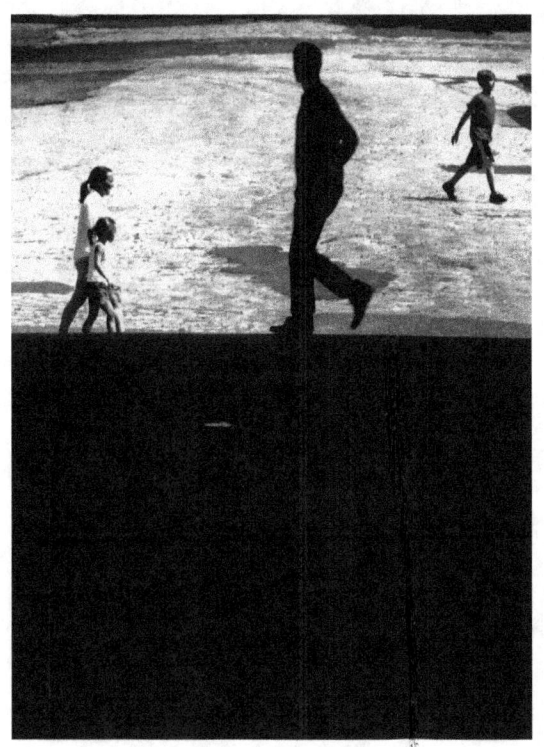 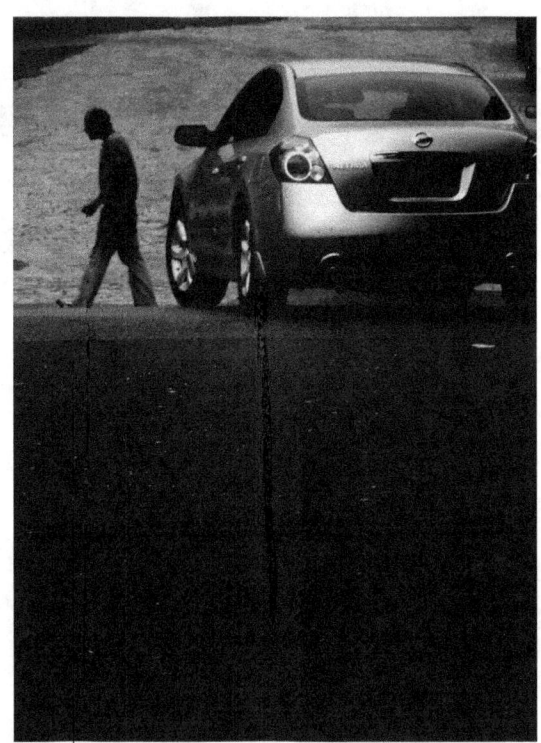

Single Shots: Minimalism, etc.

Now that you've had a look at a small fraction of the many series I am working on, the remainder of the book will consist of single images, shot at various locations around downtown Seattle. In my work, so far, you have seen a hint of minimalism in some of my images. Now you'll see the ultimate result of my quest for the effects of shadow and light, in which less is more and, in many cases, there is only the barest hint of form, revealed by shadow, silhouette and thin ribbons of rim lighting, here and there. The cover image of this book is a case in point.

There is a symbiotic relationship between darkness and light. In fact, light even creates darkness, in the form of cast shadows. There is a yin and yang relationship, in which form is simultaneously hidden and revealed and the unseen is seen, for, without light, sight is impossible and so is the photographic image. Where there is light, there must also be shadow and where shadows lurk, light is present, also. Even on an overcast day, when we often talk of "shadowless" lighting, there is actually shadow present. There must be, because light is present. Hence, the contrast between the two is there. It's simply very subtle, waiting for me to bring it out.

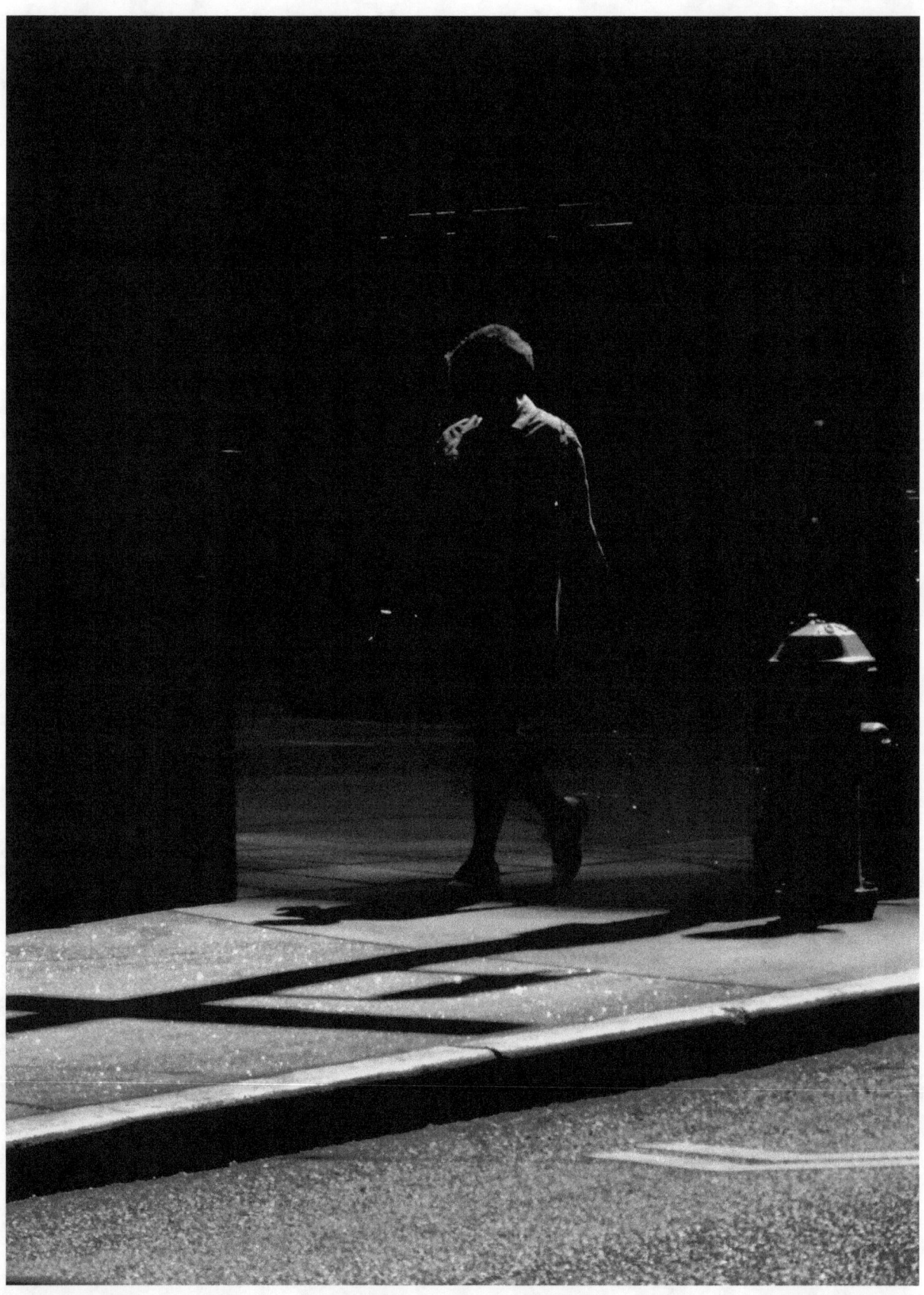

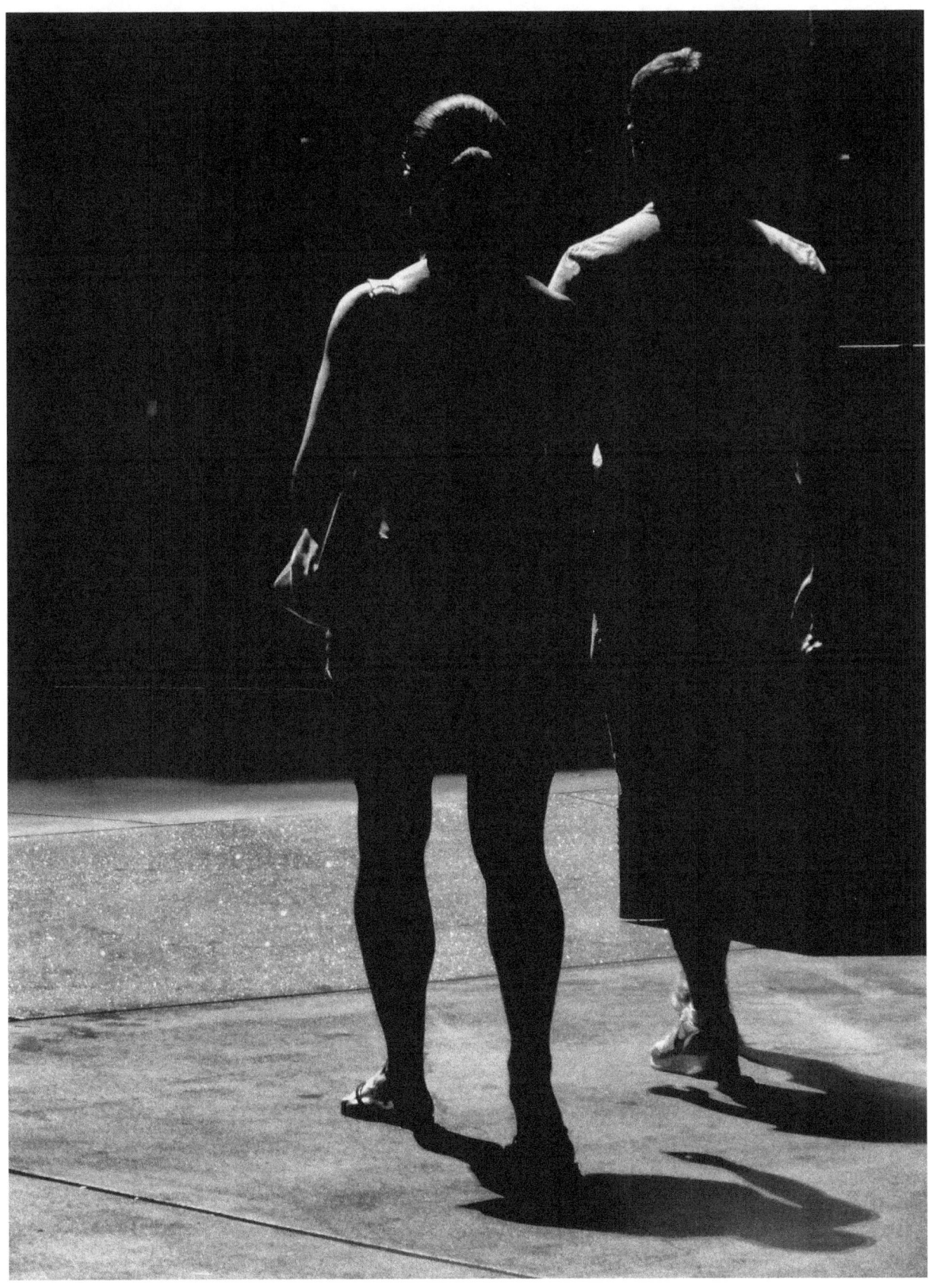

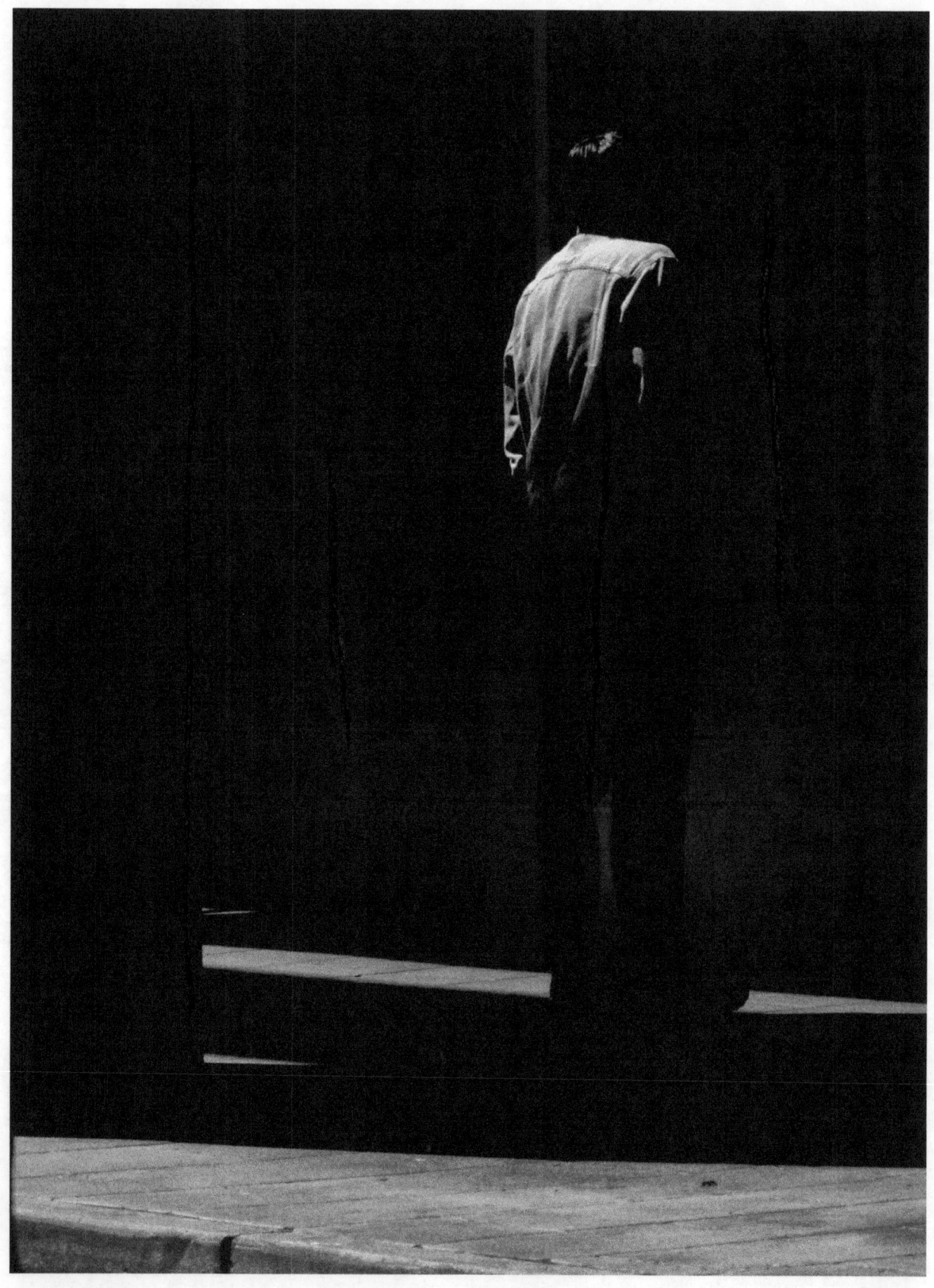

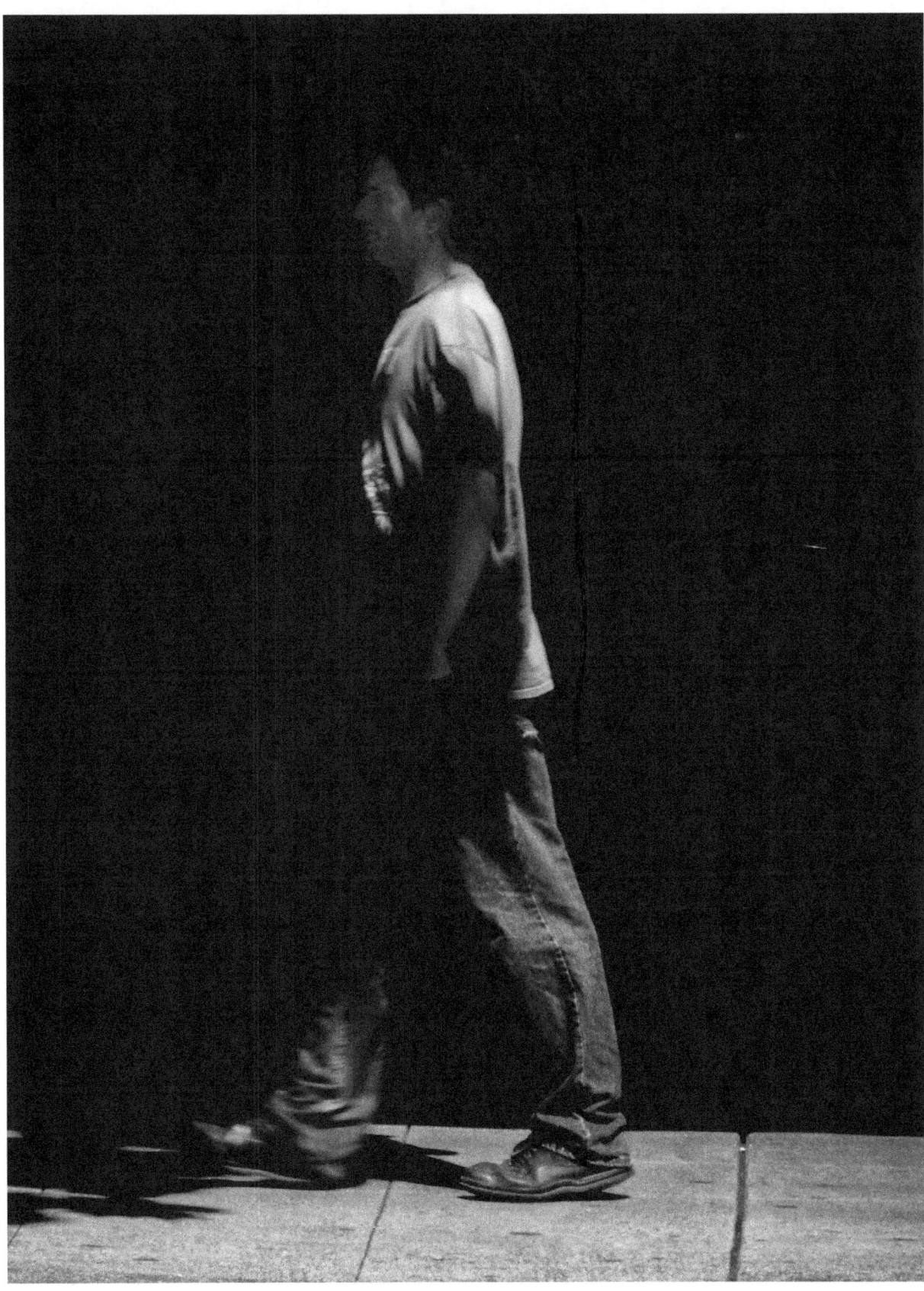

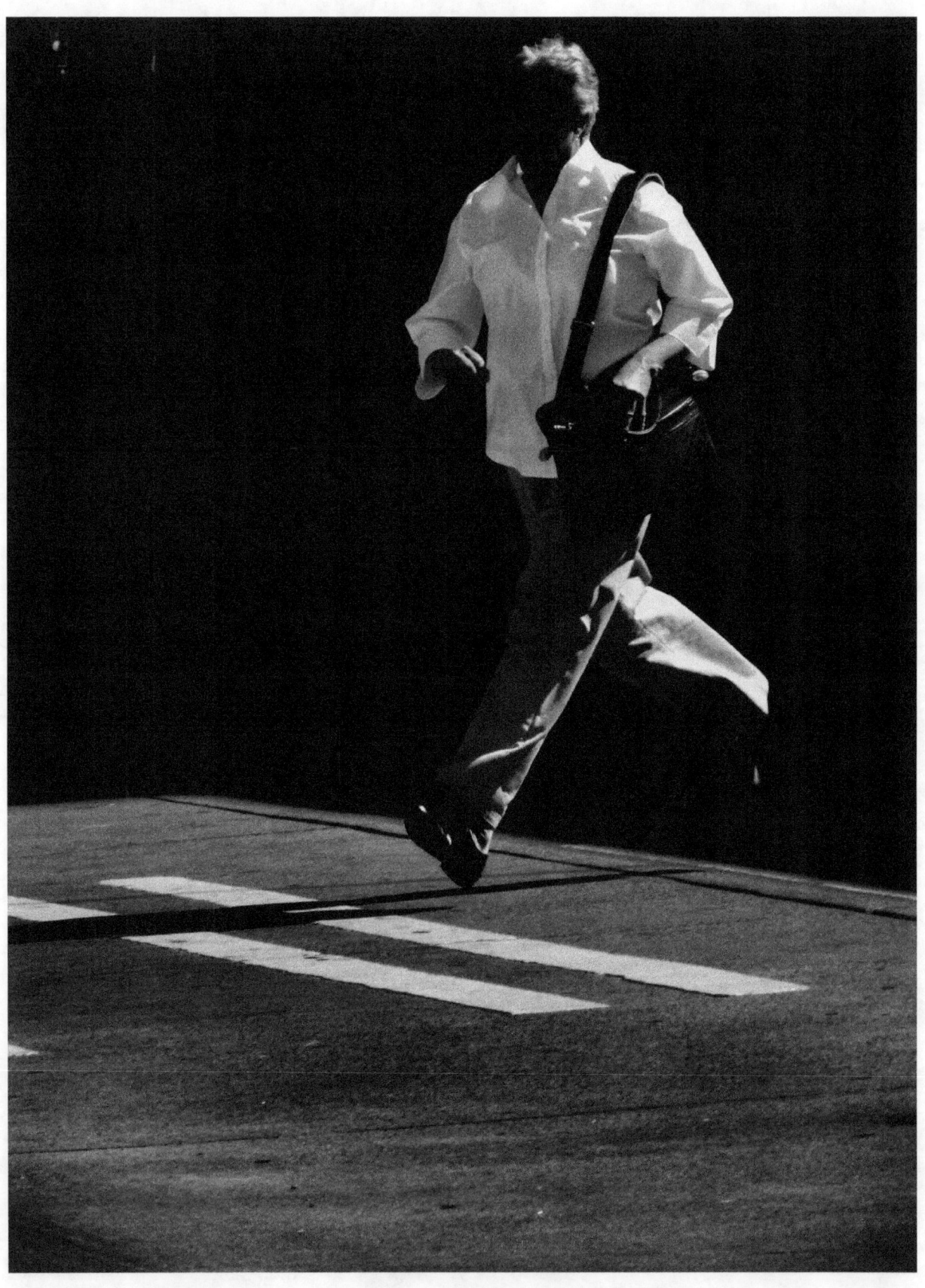

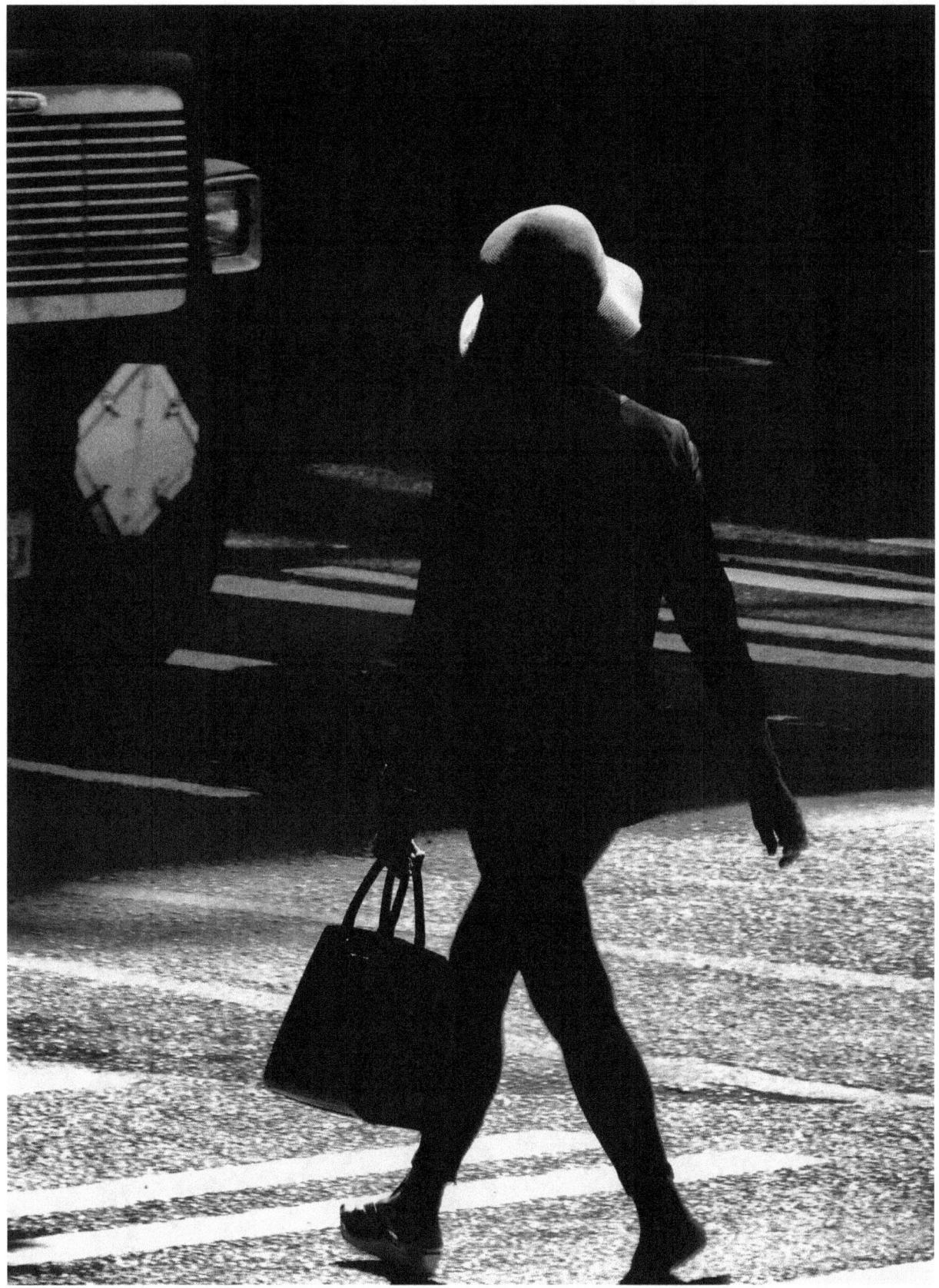

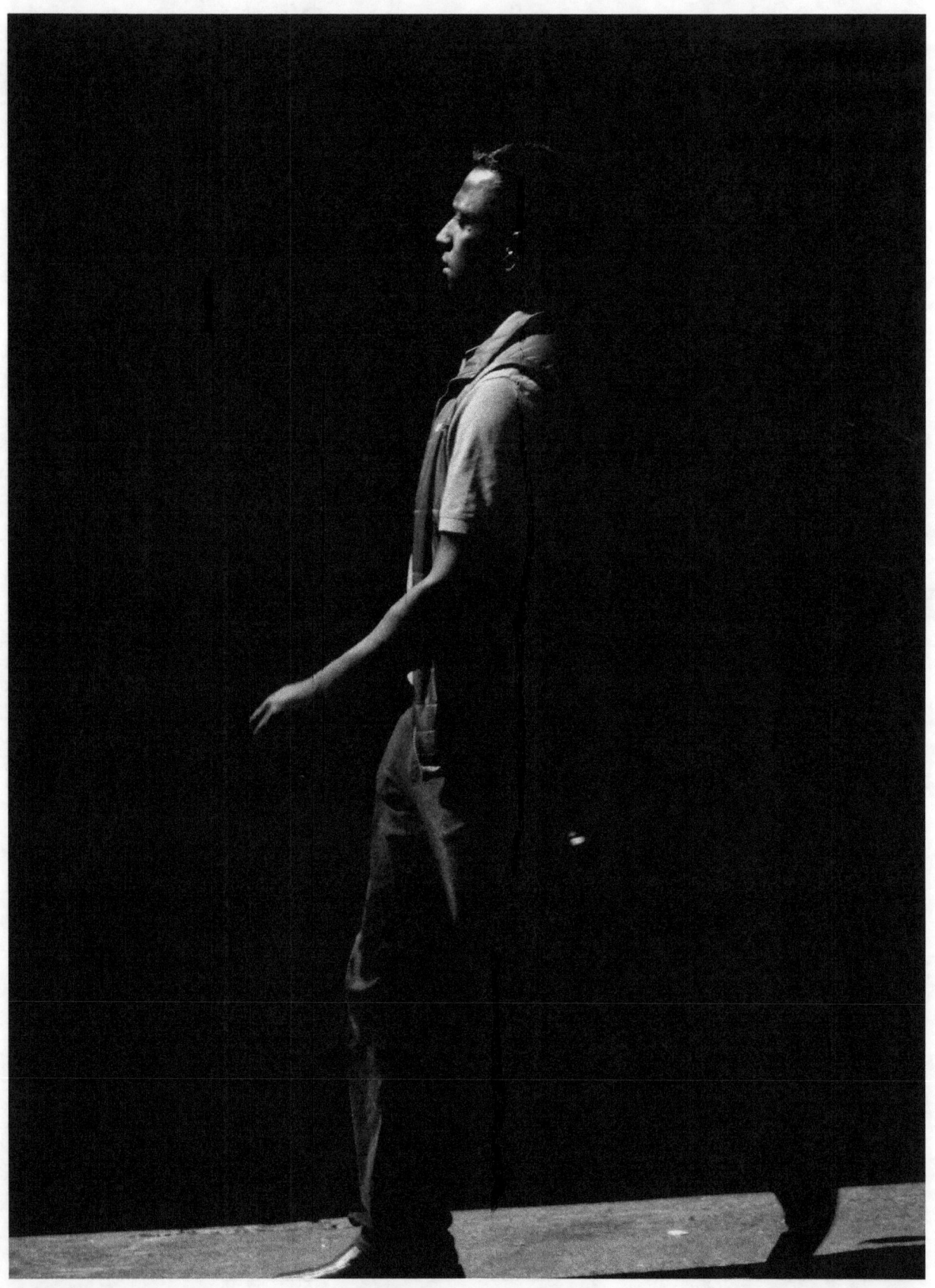

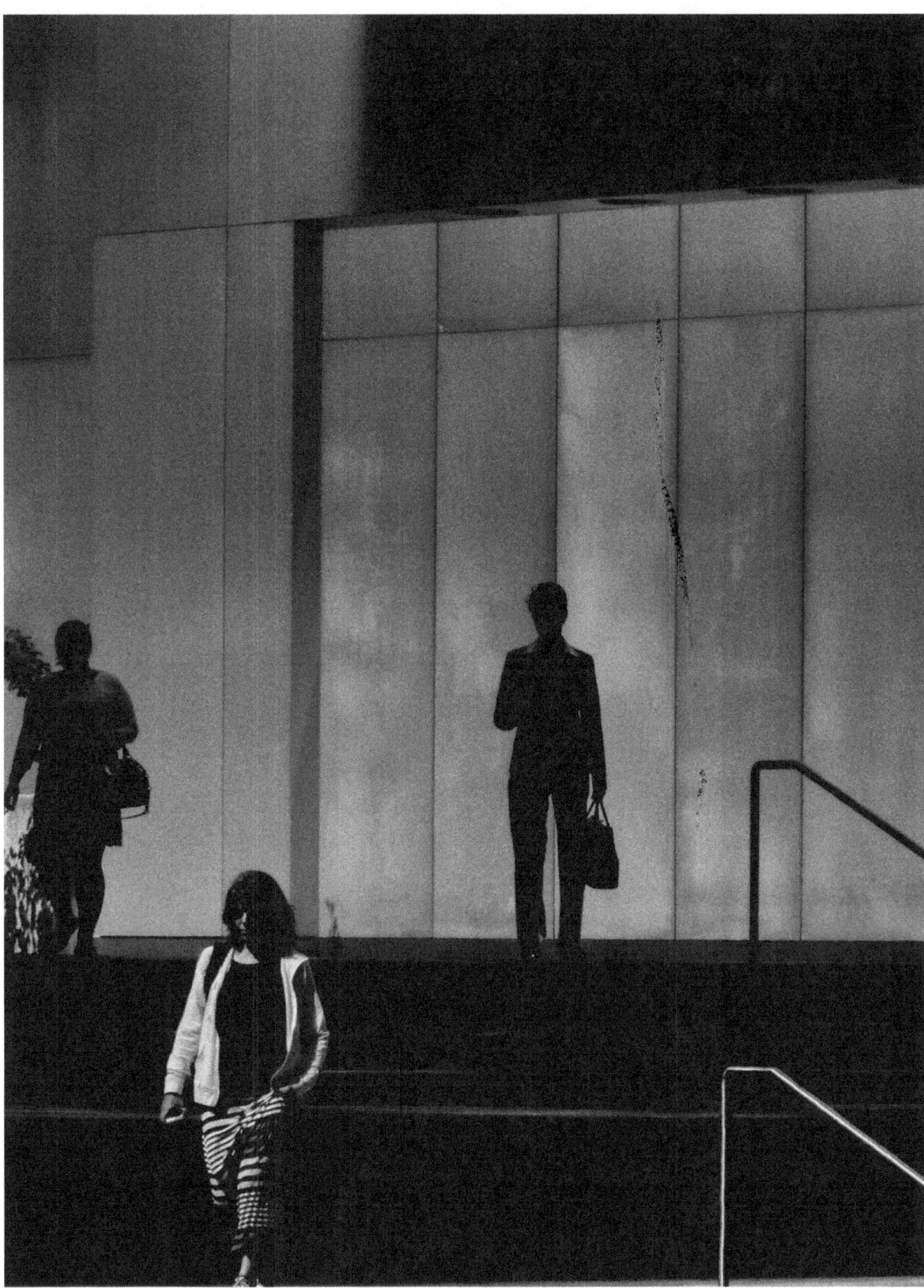

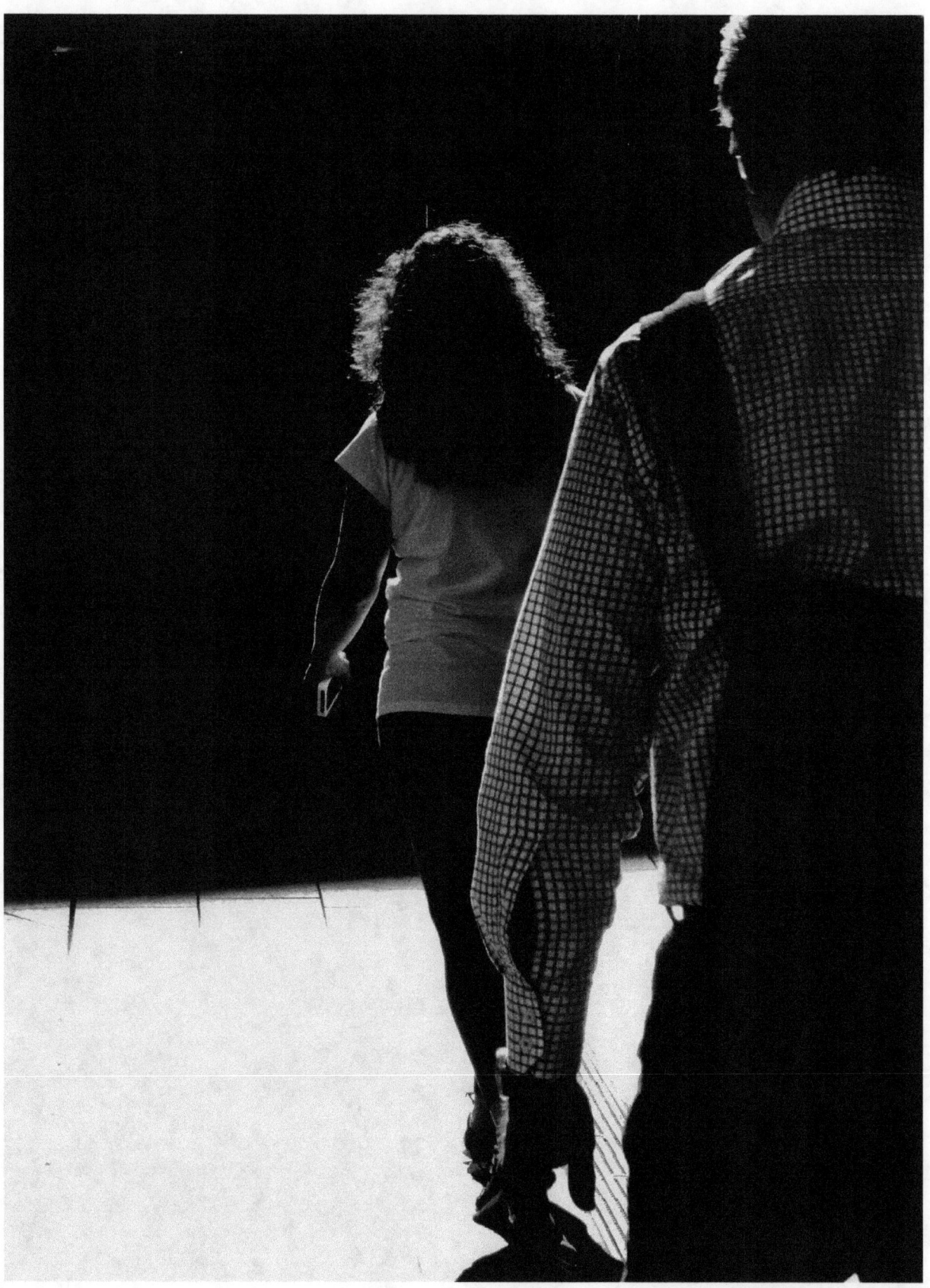

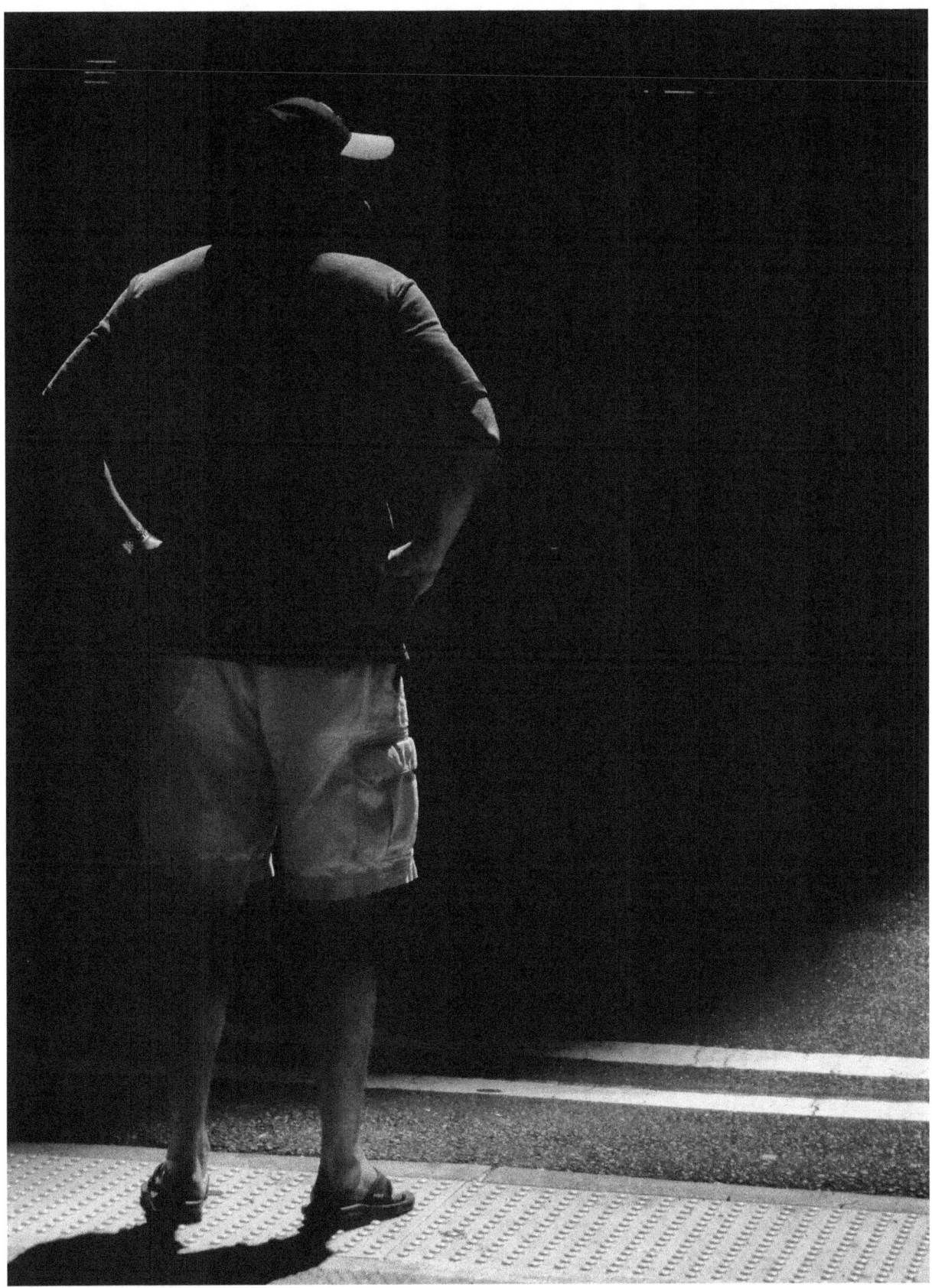

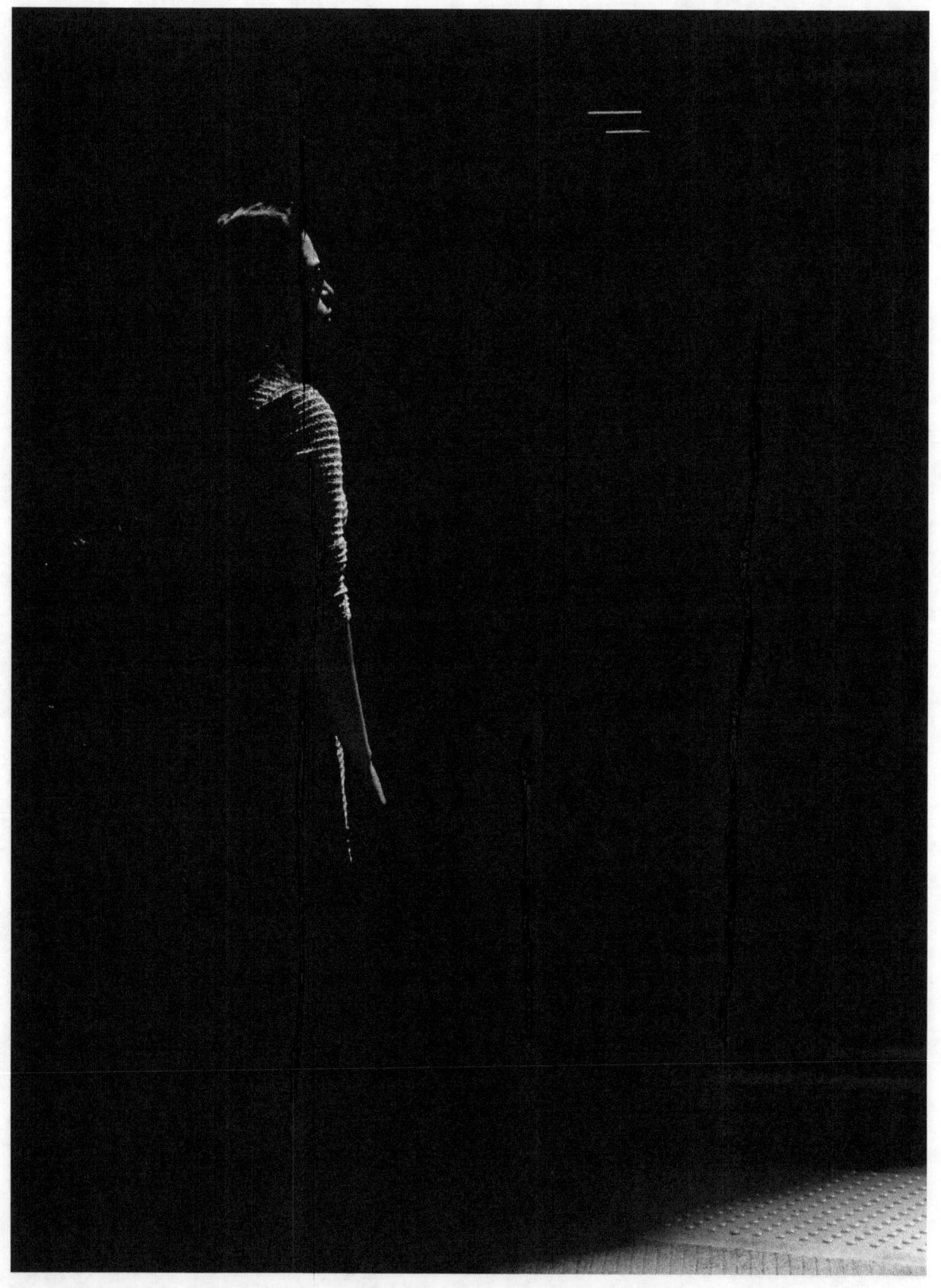

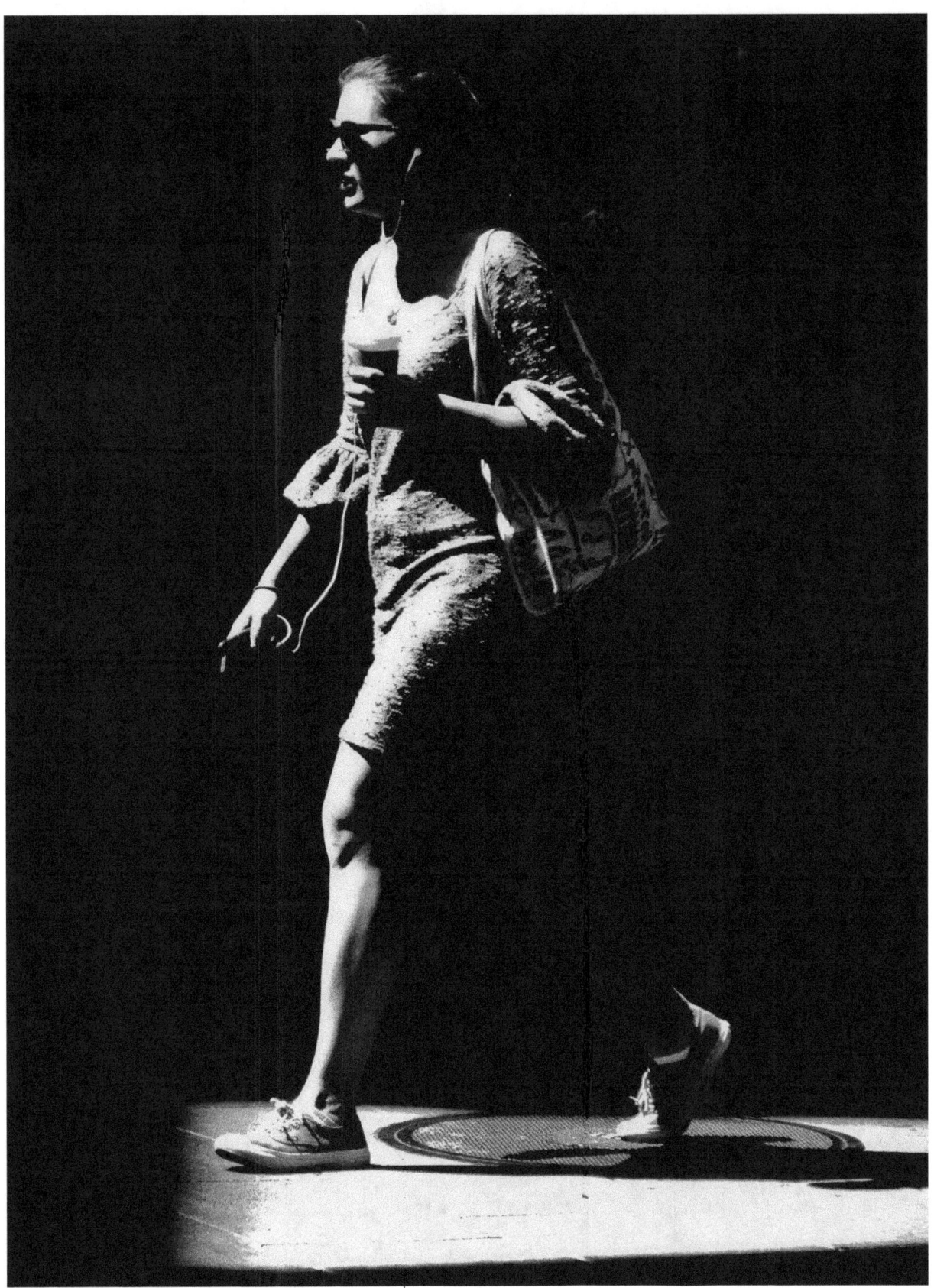

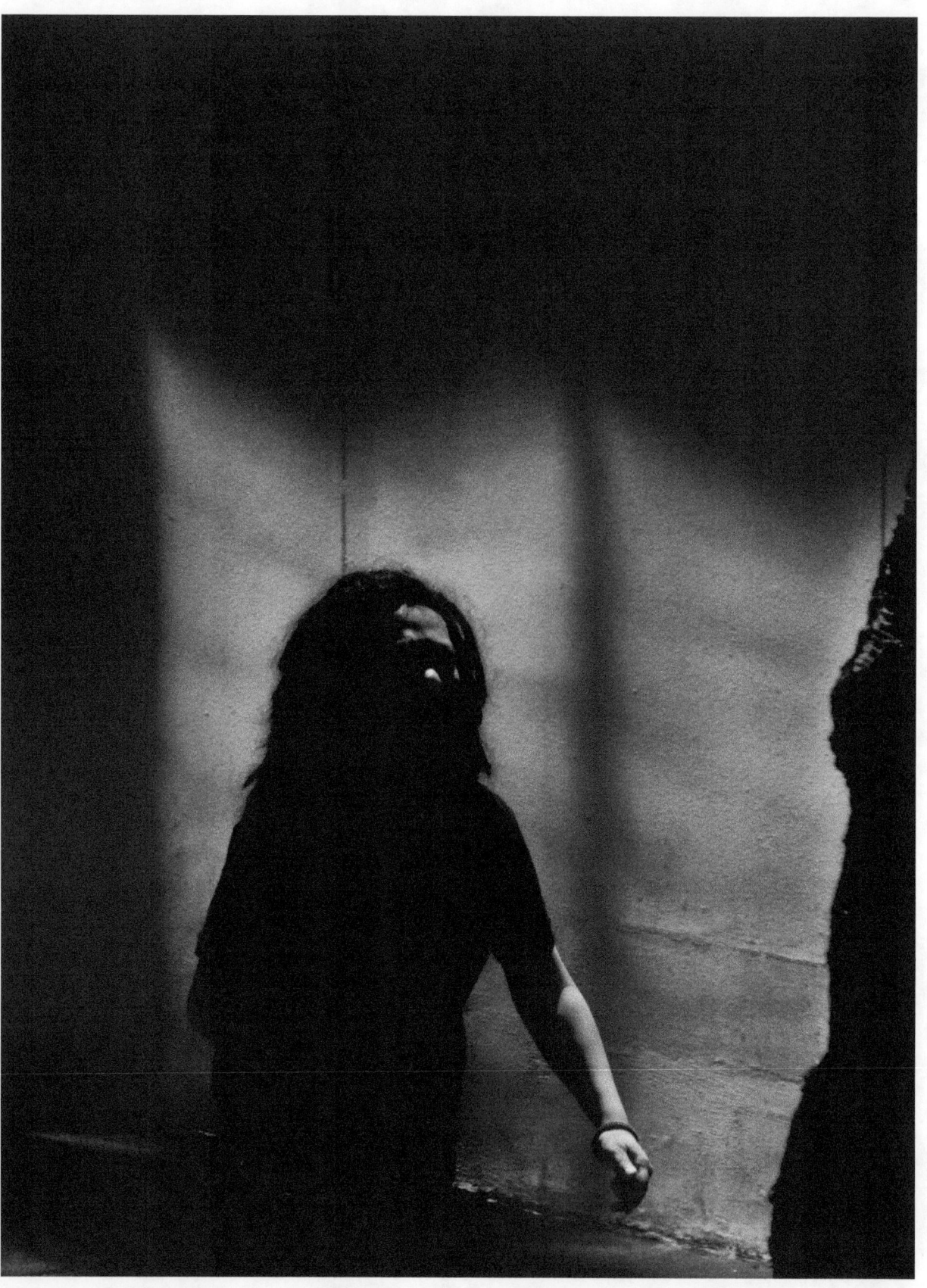

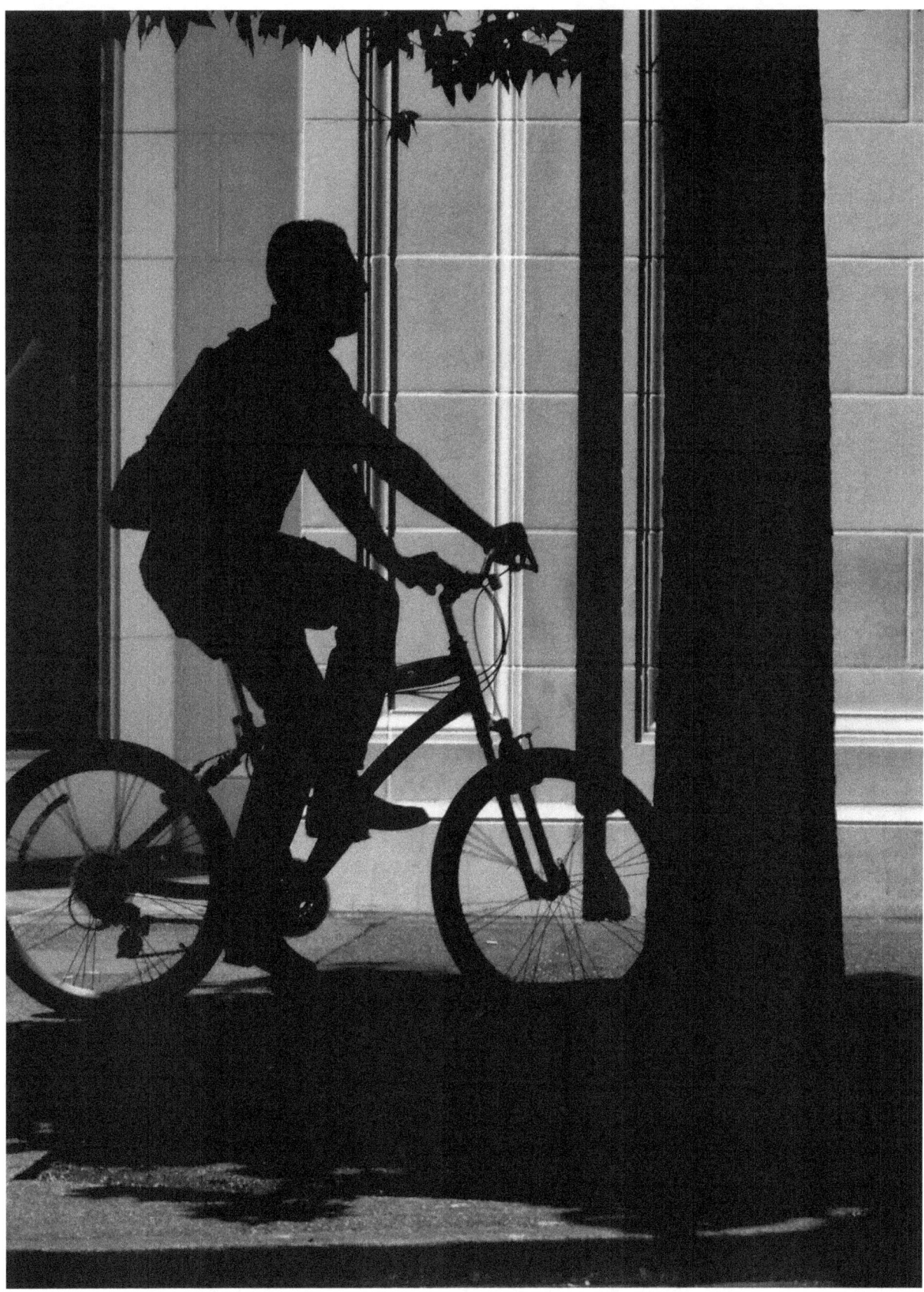

www.ingramcontent.com/pod-product-compliance
Lightning Source LLC
Chambersburg PA
CBHW080626180526
45168CB00007B/3073